So

A Second Collection of Poetry by

Martha Bible Smith

CrossHouse

Printed in the United States of America
by Lightning Source, Inc.

Unless otherwise indicated,
all Scripture taken from the Holy Bible,
New International Version, copyright 1973, 1978, 1984
by International Bible Society

Library of Congress Control Number: 2010933137
ISBN 978-1-934749-89-0

CrossHouse Publishing
P.O. Box 461592
Garland, Texas 75046
1-800-747-0738
www.crosshousepublishing.org

This book is dedicated to my son, Jon,
who shares my plane of thought,
and to my son, James,
who dares to be plain on what matters.

Table of Contents

5

Author's Note

So, simply said, I want to leave a thank-you for my nine decades. So much goodness has saturated my life. Guided by the right hand of a forgiving and sustaining Heavenly Father and tended by human hands, I have enjoyed life. Both the heavenly hand and human hands are still at work on me. My own hands have been active and passive. These poems or word piths or "prose-etry" (Marie's name for them) are that effort.

Residing at White Rock Court among the cream of old-age people reminds me of my mother's dairy product, which was changed from cream to butter and whey. We're here for another chapter in life and arrive here from different pastures. We bring memories—some to share, some to withhold. So strange that scientists now are intensely studying us. I'm sharing glimpses of personalities at their prime, so greet them.

As I have been working on this project, I am deeply aware of my husband's love of poetry. Serving on the U.S.S. Pennsylvania across the wide Pacific he carried in his pea-sized wallet a John Donne quotation. After World War II and our marriage he volunteered as a teacher in churches, mega- and family-sized. He always quoted his favorites. Quite recently one of his Sunday School men asked me to finish—

"The moving finger writes; and having writ moves on; nor all thy Piety nor Wit shall lure it back to cancel half a line— nor all thy Tears wash out a Word of it."

I found it prophetic that a 13th-century poet translated from The Rubiayat in the 19th should point its finger at 21st century and our dependence on technology.

The first poet in my life was my sister, Catherine, who taught me to read and who at 99+ still inspires me. She's Mimi, loved by many. My mother, an elocution teacher, made words dance. My teacher, Mr. W.W. Combs, wrote of an April sunset, "A lovely thing is made sublime when shared." As my family, teachers, and friends shared, I also want to share.

Thanks to the wonderful Moore family it is possible— Louis for encouraging and finding Lauren Johnson, a typist; Kay Wheeler Moore for stringing it together and editing; and to Katie Welch for her financial and artistic touch. The Richland Emeritus group encouraged me. My "Fertile Infertility" effort wasn't scorned. So, here 'tis—*So*. Please enjoy.

Martha Bible Smith

So

Just So

Poetry makes us think,
                    smile,
                    feel,
                    understand.
Poets sense a need to save moments.
                    a word
                    or two,
                    few, but just so.
Hopefully I'll be a poet—
                    just so
                    I share
                    things I care
                    about.
Poems evolve from our senses
Maybe the sixth sense is memory.

Poetry is a river
And solitude is a bridge
Through writing we cross it.
–Kaissar Afif of Lebanon,

Around the World in 80 Poems,
Selected by James Berry, Audelia Library

My Soliloquy

So

So be it.
    God's finishing words.
    Genesis
So shall it be.
    Jesus teaching.
    Matthew
So also.
    James explaining.
    New Testament
So sow . . .
    Seeds of love 'n'
    kindness.
So sew
    Seams of joy 'n'
    togetherness.
So resole
    Old shoes 'n'
    make-likenewness.
So feed your soul
    As you old.

So long,
Martha Bible Smith
8-31-16

For God So

John 3:16 begins so simply
to show
so completely
Love . . .
so inclusive
so definitive
so capably,
making
no omissions.
Even me.

So, There It'll Be

I couldn't find it
        and then I did—assurance.
I'd sung
        "Blessed assurance Jesus is mine"
        All my life it seemed.
"He redeemed", my Bible says.
Its depth became forcibly real
        in dead-of-night stillness.
Pin-dropping silence.
In a city of sixty-million people.
        Yet alone.
The wisp of a white cloud
        whispered against sky's darkest blue.
My lonely blues and downs
        weren't there anymore.
So, I won't lose it. I hid
        assurance in my soul.
There, it'll be.

Dimensions of God's Love

So wide only
      the sun can enfold
So long as
      the earth's axis spins
So high that
      the sky's the limit
So deep like
      the sea, reaching forever.

So Strange

A wee plastic statue of St. Francis of Assissi
Stands in my wee balcony garden.
Miniature bird on his shoulder
With food for real birds at his feet.
So strange how words of others affect us.
For years my Sunday School yearbook
Made his prayer our class prayer.

  "Lord, make me an instrument of thy Peace
  Where there is hatred, let me sew love;
  Where there is injury, pardon;
  Where there is doubt, faith;
  Where there is despair, hope;
  Where there is darkness, light;
  Where there is sadness, joy."

Now, years later the prayer is there
Where it withstands wear—sun, wind, rain, snow.
St. Francis, wherever you are,
You make me aware
Where there is instrument need.

Questions
How So?

To: Billy Graham, father of five
You trusted God to help Ruth raise them.
How so?

Ans: My call was from God. I hated being away,
but God's way. Ruth and God. True Partners.

To: Barbara Bush, mother of five
You trusted George.
Away for U.S.A.
Dedicated statesman.
How so?

Ans: My love was forever. George had promised
wherever he is, I am. We're true partners.

So, family matters.

Surgery, God's Art

Surgery is sometimes urgent.
       purging,
       incisive.
Yes, a must for
       correcting disease
       or brokenness.
Often, it's selective,
       electing change
       for the better.
More often, it's life's hope
       improved
       sustained
       or supported.
Surgery is human ability,
       aimed at body parts,
       all showing God's art.

Shadows

Night
The wall is bleak
Just there.
But in time,
the moon rises
Soft beams make
shadows of other walls
nearby.
Morning
The wall is bleak
Just bare
But, punctually
the sun rises.
Strong beams cast
shadows of silhouettes,
moving life.
Ecstasy
A shadow darts
With pointed beak
seeking nectar.
A calendar projection,
First hummingbird
of season returns.
Welcome this
Miracle of nature.

Hummingbirds

Their little machine bodies hum
Every movement a zinging one
Whirring, even in one spot in space,
Zooming into flowers for nectar,
Then shooting upward and away. Red, their favorite
color, nectar, drink of the gods, their fare
So, we tempt them.
Just sugared H2O.
They respond to give a glimpse
Of ruby throats, peacock
Blue wings.
Tiny. Small. Pinpoint brains
Yet, speed immeasurable,
intuitiveness beyond our comprehension.
Does the drink of the gods make the hum?
No, they humble us as God's powerful Creation.

The Election 2008

Being a prudent voter in 2008
Requires thumping the slate.
Since grade school when we had
        current events weekly,
I've been interested in the times.
These times seem spent.
It's hard to discern the current
        of events.
So, what must I do?
Vote, by all means, after study.
        Test for the best.
Not the polls. Not the broken goals.
My gumption says—
Our founding fathers looked way ahead.
        "Change," they said.
        So we go to vote.

Barack Obama's Mother

First, her parents wanted a son
So she was given Stanley Ann Dunham
Which became S. Ann Dunham.
A Kansas native, moved as a teen to Hawaii.
Teen pregnancy and marriage
to Barack Obama of Kenya.
Divorce.
Next, fearless, she departed for Indonesia.
Name Ann Soetoro.
Another divorce and a Ph.D.
Not lacking security,
his maternal grandmother in Hawaii nurtured.
Madelyn Dunham gave love unconditional.
Following Barbara Bush as First Mother,
Ann gave a questing intelligence
and problem-solving skills—
Significant for our present President.

The Thinker

Rodin sculpted his man of thought in 1880,
Inspired, no doubt, by Dante's writing of 1330:
"Consider your origins: you were not born
that you might live as brutes but
so as to follow virtue and knowledge" XXVI 118

In 1950 in D.C. I bought a pair of bookends,
Plaster but supposedly a scale model
of the sculpture, bronze, and marble in museum.
My sister had bulging shelves of books
so one of the pair was a gift to her.
The one I kept tumbled, broke into three pieces.
When glued, "he" seemed slow to think on my desk.

In 1960 in Dallas, Texas, a life-sized resin model
showed up in a nearby shop.
Bartering some of my husband's merchandise (jewelry)
"he" became mine. Yes, full-sized replica.
A moving van delivered to our porch.
The B. Poarches, neighbors, gaped.
"Martha's daft," my husband explained then, and often.

Years "he" spent in our den.
Just thinking, supporting his chin on his wrist,
and his arm on his knee.
Our sons poked fun often, sometimes defended to kids
Seeing the original at Rodin's tomb in the Musee
Sister and I stood speechless. We just thought.

No wonder "he's" revered internationally.

When my teaching career said, "Retire",
My sister's idea was for "the thinker"
to change places. He should go to a campus
of my beloved Garland schools. She arranged.
Then, my son, Jon, suggests "him" for the cover.
A sun dial from outside for *Yet*. So appropriate.
Hopefully, my take on this masterpiece is a thought.

April 17, 1944
Washington, D.C.

Here I am, with a Mississippi accent or accident,
teacher-trained, yet working for
The Ordnance Department, U.S. Army.
Truthfully ignorant about ammunition
And weapons of war. Pentagon.

But World War II has changed
So much for so many—men, women, and
Even more for children.
Upheaval, transplants, unknown destinations.
Nothing's the same or ever will be. Defense.

This city is abloom in cherry pink.
The Japanese ornamental trees announce spring.
What is this? We're at war with Japan.
How could two nations with past
"good-will" be at dagger points? An attack.

It's harder to understand than
My being a civil servant researcher.
Comprehend the whys and purposes
Of nation conflict? It's far and away
Too much, too deep, too distressing. History.

But on this beautiful spring day
I'm lavishing in beauty I never dreamed to see
Of trees, gifted to our nation by the
Nation, now our foe.
So unseemly, so disparate, so unhuman. April.

Beauty preceded war.
War can't thwart the beauty
Beauty has its own path
Even nations pause and thaw with awe.

Note: Mrs. Helen Taft, our First Lady in
1912, had planted two and then thousands as gifts to
U.S.A.

For Us

'Twas promised—
a savior
'Twas called
believing
'Twill relieve
unsteadiness
'Tweren't no lie.
Jesus came to die.
All for us.
'Twon't go away.
Fall no more.
'Twas done.

On My Walls

Grant Woods' 1932 "Spring Ploughing"
and a picture of Daddy hoeing
our garden are not just decor
for me.

In a material form they show the
reality and beauty of man's unison with
NATURE

Artists and authors have themed through
the ages man's work in
NATURE.

Historians and philosophers spent
their years searching for man's
NATURE.

My 94 years only say to me,
"Early childhood found your
lifetime companion in
NATURE."

"The kiss of the sun for pardon
The song of the birds for mirth
One is nearer God's heart in a garden
Than anywhere else on earth."
–Dorothy Gurney, 1858-1932

Sow

Job's Wife

In a dramatic poem in the Old Testament
    We meet a nuclear family of
    husband, wife, seven sons, three daughters.
    Closely knit, much camaraderie.
Job is a testament of man's humanity
    And God's sovereignty.
Wealthy, influential, most important
    He honored God.
In the East no man was equal in status.
A challenge was flung from Satan to God.
    Test him.
    Thus began the testing.
Calamity. Loss. One fell swoop—
    Children, homes, servants, animals, health.
    Gone.
Job was left with his wife and his faith.
Only a Greek translation gives his wife's name
    Dinah.
Much time lapsed. Isn't honor due
    The wife who dost remain?
Were the seven sons and three beautiful daughters—
Job's reward—hers too?
    I think so.
    Yes, hers too.

Jemimah, Keziah, and Keren-Happuch named
Declared the most beautiful in the land
What a life for a nameless wife.
    And there were
    Son's sons too.

Parenting

The child's soap bubble
Lasts only a moment.
Firmly round, colorful, and fragile.

Growing larger
Floating away
Bursting.
No sound.
The child is so lovable.
Early years only a sweet scent
Mischief-bound, ever playful, and agile.

Growing into teen
Slipping away,
Thirsting for love,
No ground.

Keeping a child lovable
is a parenting bubble
Floating away so gradually.

Women

We are women.
   We care.
We nurture.
   We are
   Daughters
   Sisters
   Aunts
   Wives
   Mothers
   Mothers-in-law
   Stepmothers
   Exes
   Widows
   Grandmothers
   Great-grandmothers
   Cousins
   Friends.
We are feminine.
   Pride in being so.
So, did you know
a 19th-century well-known thinker
identified "memory"
as feminine?
"She, the brain, is essential."
   So are women.

Woman Carry Gene

Woman carry gene. Woman
Bear child. Woman
Rear family. Woman
Fear atom. Woman
Gears search. Woman
Hears God. Woman
Leery evil. Woman
Tears shed. Woman
God's vessel.

*Apologies to Gwendolyn Brooks, one year
my junior, yet Pulitzer-Prize winner. Her
"We Real Cool" is a perceptive view of her
culture. As an infertile woman I find God
honors woman's place throughout His Word.*

Waiting to Bloom

Night-Blooming Cereus
Like being serious
About what matters.

The pot above your head
Is the plant so named.

It is scraggly
But it survives
Whatever the weather.

You're like a night-blooming cereus
When, much anticipated, you bloom.

Your blossom will be awesome.
Pink stem leading to luscious white fibers
Delicate with an overwhelming
      aroma.
Kristina, I'm waiting for your bloom,
      A loving Gma.

Search for Significance

Found only partly in her resume
    B.S. from University of Mississippi
    Ph.D. University of North Carolina
    2nd degrees
    Massachusetts Inst. Technology
    Leadership in Sloan's School
        Of Business
        And
Commendation from
National Aeronautics Space Agency.

But decidedly in
    Her pattern of daily living
    And care for others.
Examples:
    Helen Adams, her mother-in-law's
        Alzheimers
    Cordis Corbin, her grandson's
        Autism
Me, her aunt, slow-learner in finance.
Zounds! Belinda, my beloved niece.

Lu's Accident
High School Graduation
May 19

So—a no answer.
The situation was critical
A precious daughter's life
Endangered. Loss of blood.
Bone damage. Changed priorities.
Grandparents' care rearranged.
Doctors delay bone surgery.
"It is best because she makes
new bone slowly."
Mother's question, "Did my laxness
On stressing milk cause?"
Doctor's reply, "No. Do you know
any animal that drinks milk
after it's weaned?"

Two Stars

Your first two grands
Become your pride and joy.
Pride is kin to arrogance
But Joy is love's alloy.

Wherever they went
Eyes seemed to follow.
She, with shiny red hair
      fair skin and statuesque walk.
He, the picture of health
      disguising a breathing problem.
Me, the beaming grandmother
      cherishing every moment.

I purchased outfits
Matching blue/white, just right.
Made date at Kim's Modeling agency
So, with their chic mom
We go for auditions.

As it turned, I had three candidates.
Their mom charmed the judges too.
Contracts for three? Wait and see.
Only Bryant was called for Easter ad,
His broken arms in casts canceled.

Alys carried the basket
For egg-hunting at our
Family gathering.

Fast-forward 25 years.

Alys, bridesmaid baker's dozen times,
Still modelish in executive offices,
Loyal to her church with voice,
Always available aunt to four.

Bryant, basketball and playboy style aside
Found Jennifer, mother of two. Cottage wedding.
Maturity force-fed by Lauren, Elaine
Then, Taylor and Landen, proudest father ever.
Grandmother, two stars and more pride and joy.

Waiting to be a Bride

My granddaughter Alys
seemed shy in childhood,
aloof to boys as a teen,
nonchalant through her 20s—
marriage not her thing.

Quite debonair
with her Mom's style for flair
and her Dad's red hair,
she'd just enjoy brother's
find—a single mom with two
achieving, Lauren and Elaine.

Even the arrival of Taylor,
niece with eyes like hers, and
nephew, image of his dad,
didn't whet her desire
for coupling with someone.

But, at church she found
working with Jay Dill
quite pleasant, easy
conversation shared interests.
He'd recently divorced.
He had joint custody of three
Jayce, 9, Hailey, 8, and Bryce, 5.

Seeing them with their dad
charmed her.

Soon they were having fun together.
So, at Christmas 2008
the rest of the family met Jay and his three.
To plan her wedding she'd
use bits of the many
weddings she'd attended and been a part of.

The invitation for March 20, 2010
at five at Paradise Cove outside
on Grapevine's lake just at twilight.
Blustery, wintry, disturbing weather
moved the nuptial inside—
perhaps for better appreciation of
her childhood pastor's challenge.
Following Jay's and Alys's vow exchange,
Rev. Cavin asked the children to form
a circle with their Dad and Alys.

A crystal vase was empty.
Vials of sand were given Jay and Alys.
Pour in. Shake. Blend. Beautiful mix.
Then to each child a vial of sand
        to contribute.
Shake. Blend. Bigger and better.
Then a vial of white sand representing Christ
was added.
Shake. Blend. A Christian family pronounced.

The many guests enjoyed
the couple's inclusive sharing
of joy. Seven children,
unusual foods, music from
Jay's bands and a heavenly
sent blessing—so meaningful.
Snowflakes, inch-sized, were
falling as guests and family departed.
"Alys, affirmation of who you are,
waiting to be a bride has a
storybook ending, we pray."
So they lived happily
Ever after.

So, Upon My Soul

Surprise! Yes!
Who'd have thought it?
My goodness!
You didn't just sit.
You did it.

Upon my soul!
Child, look at you!
You're out of the hole!
Ain't no joke. True.
Credit-card debt no more.
A believe-it-or-not.
Year 2009. Depression.

Psalm V, I

Give ear to my words, O Lord,
Consider my meditation.

(KJV)

Your ear, Lord
    My words
    My efforts
    My meditation.

Please hear, Lord,
    My cries
    My stumbles
    My humble plea.

Consider my flawed life.
Reconsider my broken focus.
Give me another chance.
Call my name again.
Make my deaf ears to hear
If only what you say—
So-o-o-o important.
Like clearing new ground.
Sow a new crop of deeds.

Dear God,

Is this return
home bringing two
children my
second chance?
I'm tired.
I'm deaf.
I'm the one
who needs care.
Please make
it clear to me
what I should
do about each
family member.

—Martha

Dear God,
Please help James
to realize what he
is doing for us.

—His Mother

So, My Son

So, I make a request
only one chapter
from one follower
to another about
being apart.
"It may be that
my time away
from you for
a short time
was so
that you might
have him back for
all time."
Philemon
KJV

So, prophetic for my son and me.
A four-year absence made it so.

Lost Children

Every mall provides for lost children.
Parents are so glad.
Alys and Bryant were ours
On weekends for several hours.
Collin Creek Mall was new then.
Their granddad was beginning to weaken.
So we'd eat food treat
He'd people-watch from his seat
Toys, pets, books—anything for our whim
Go back near closing time for him.
An empty bench? Oh my!
Where's Granddad?
Searched and searched.
Do they provide for lost Grands?
Children would be so glad.

He's on a bench at another level.

January 22, 2007 2:00am

Dear God,

> Today is Jon's birthday.
> Thank you for giving him to me.
> Thank you for this love and life.
> Today he stated he and Karen
> The friendship-to-love relationship
> They've had for years
> That's a courthouse JP visit
> To make them one.
>
> No ado.
> No family present.
> Only witnesses and
> Karen and Jon
> Saying, "I do."
> Fervent, for them.

Dear God,

> Bless this union
> Give constancy.
> Oneness, endearing,
> Embracing each other and You.

> *Martha*

In His Heart

It was my son who said
  "There is no God."
The baby who'd been dedicated to God
  at birth
The child who'd been educated
  at church and VBS
The teen who'd brought his friends
  to camp, choir, and carnivals.
The adult who began to drop
  God's name in vain.
The young parent who let Gma
  do the taking to Sunday School.
The split couple who began to fight over
  bills, thrills, and alcohol.
The dysfunctional extended family blaming
  each other.
It was a life asunder.
Parents and son hear the thunder.
Wait . . . Wait . . . Wait . . . There are promises.
The weight of forgiveness was borne
  by a SON.
Ask for it, son. It begins in the heart.
                              Psalm 14:3

Just Hands Off

Then, quite unexpectedly
They appear—My heart stops.
They've matured.
     They're on a new page.
     I'm not an old fixture.
     I'm a bit of a sage.
Yes, I stood
Again with my former pastor.
He, too, had had a turn-a-way.
After greeting each other fondly
I said, "It did hold."
Yes, today, in our church a renewal.
For them, for me, and for him.

My Anchor Holds

So, apart—Separated for four years
No word. No exchange. Only prayer.
Rambunctious, defiant, tempted,
A terrible experimental time. Helpless I felt.
Turning 90 years in the meantime.
Not only deaf to fellow residents but also
     beloved child.
My still, small voice had said,
     "Take hands off
     both son and his two."
Finding me, they came with
     changed attitudes.
To cement renewal they wanted
     church attendance together.
Familiar song, "My Anchor Holds".
Our pastor, he, too, with a turn-away son
said, "Foundation held." Strong words.

So, Summer Solstice 2009

Dear James,

Your planning
for the end of
four years apart was perfect.
I knew it
would eventually end
because of
prayer and promise.
So, when in just one day
questions were answered,
Reunion—
Better than a dream.
Yes, for real. Let's seal it.

Love,
Mother

Confirmed

Love sank in.
Yes, it's 2010.
Mimi's bank
of prayers and
hugs for my J's
paid.
Now, each has
a wife to love.

True love will never come undone
It is as big as all eternity
and higher than the sun.
Jesse Stewart, "Autumn Lovesong"

Sew

BI-O-BITZ
White Rock Court Anthology

In the Dallas-Fort Worth area, Gracious Living or Retirement homes are numerous. Before you elect to join one, you make a search and visit several. When one seems to fit your lifestyle, your family helps you settle in. Doing so requires giving away or disposing of decades of memories, mementos, collections, and furnishings. One must also terminate utilities, security systems, mail delivery, and connections for phone, TV, and computers. The most used term for this is "downsizing". This, of course, follows either selling or re-titling one's homeplace to someone else.

Then, after beginning your new life, you visit other such homes of your friends and inadvertently compare and observe customs and people. I was a visitor for a gourmet luncheon at a coveted facility. Arriving at the gated, beautifully-architectured home of my friend, I was seated in a well-appointed lobby while I awaited our assembly. A litany, I observed. Yes, it was just that, a dreary, repetitive occurrence. And it spoke to me with significance.

A stack of local newspapers was available for the perusal of tenants. From my comfortable Williamsburg chair, with a mirror-defined wall, I saw them come and pick up the Dallas Morning News, Fort Worth Star Telegram, or another. Each person turned first to the obituary column without even glancing at the headlines.

Were my eyes deceiving me? I mentioned this at lunch; others said, "Yes, I do it too." Why, oh my, why? At this the rarest stage in our lives are we morose, morbid, or mopey to the Nth degree?

Break us awake! Take the cake!

Make us quake! For gosh sakes!

Obituary says, "It's over."

"It isn't over until the fat lady sings," according to Yogi Berra. It isn't over until taps is playing in the military. It isn't over until the Christian benediction, "Alleluia Amen." It isn't over until the Catholic Requiem, "Grant them rest eternal."

So I think prior to an obituary there should be wonderful sharing of bios. My offering is "bi-o-bitz"—lives of residents still inspiring. Unlike "Spoon River Anthology" by Edgar Lee Masters, I'm seeking living acclaim, not "o-bit" or "a-bit-o'-life".

Geoffrey Chaucer, in the Canterbury Tales printed in the end of the 15th century, showed us that lives had diversity but also revealed common needs for love and joy in daily living. So in this early century with its many complexities, a look at life before death is revealing.

Time for Us

White Rock leaves time
to retrieve
Sleeves from our past
and savor today.
Taste each moment.
The flavor will last.

Our arms aren't bare.
Short, puffed, or split-
sleeves stay the sun.
No harm just to bask
in the days of old.

Memory relived
Escapes boredom
and ennui.
We *ah* at life.

Live Oak

I know this beloved tree well.
It's my show and tell . . .
Small limbs harbor birds.
Squirrels skin its wormed trunk,
Just as if it were in a dell.

My balcony, my room with a sky roof,
Nears the live oak with proof,
God urges me to hear (though I'm deaf)—
Be aware of growth and changes.
He leads so I won't goof.

On December 12, 2008, flakes of snow fell
Dusted our live oak very well
An unbelievable beauty—
Our residents marveled at the scene
The live oak gave life to our white-haired selves.

So, Last Years

We read ads for
   "Gracious Living
   Spacious Surrounds
   Capacious Floor Space
   Delicious Meals."
Our kids hear
   "Assure your Mom or Dad care 24/7."
So with them
   "Find the fit for you."
Do downsize
   "Sell some. Then, give
   to appreciators,
   family or not."
The right-size new address
   will put you on your own,
   a lifestyle, maybe forlorn
   at first.
You'll need to weed old habits
   Routine'll change
   Mailbox'll often be empty
   Flowers'll not be from your yard
   Menus'll vary—seldom simple.

For the declined years, I've found
a chance to rewind my days
and enjoy these new friends and ways.

"So at a knock
I emptied my cage
To hide in the world
And alter with age"
–Robert Frost
1874-1963

Door Messages

To keep season themes numbered
Each wears a wreath on the door.

Some choose a one-time
"Life is fragile, handle with care."
Most invest in day welcome.
On occasion, celebrants
reflect moods or occasions.

We've seen tiny posies
and vast baskets,
baby shoes, Easter bunnies,
Christmas nativities
and Valentines galore.

Bertha, our 100-year-old
Proclaimed "Through My Century",
a published autobiography.

Carl, only 99, whose "with-it"
lifestyle was gifted with origami
colors and patterns, "fit in"
for Wilma also.

Bob, the computer genius
printed "I'm confused. Wait.
Maybe I'm not." Appropriate for all.
To keep reason we scheme
to celebrate our encumbered lives a little
more.

Kathie Sullivan
Enrichment Coordinator

Nowhere else in the world is there another—
  She's our pearl
Her stories, collected far and wide,
  show her perceptive side.
Her music, solo or chorus, directing bells,
  sounds harmonic.
Her decorations, events or season,
  turn our home into a celebration.
Her out-and-about bus takes us
  thru treed streets or traffic wild.
Her exercise, games, and crafts
  are quality time-treasured.
Her bio boasts well fame, romance and
  marriage—winsome he was
  to win her.
Her two musical daughters we also claim.
Her "OK, kiddos, it's time to go,"
  to us oldies
  enriches daily

"A fabric suture done
Readily emancipates 8+1"
Her rephrase of the familiar
"A stitch in time saves 9"

Our Honey Bee

Lee, often we say Lee G
to honor her French name, Gaynier—
She's our honey bee
flying to someone's need
because she sensed a dearth.
Keeping seniors like us
on an even keel—
is just what her pollen does.
She found the best in many a test
along the way. Time for a rest
found her touching brush to china,
Haviland's French. Her strokes gave life
to her childhood memories—chickens.
for another plate, dessert—no—no
Hers is a date with Glen Beck, Fox.
We're glad her hive was White Rock with us.

Graven Faces

Sitting among a senior audience
Gathered to pay loving memory
    to one of our own,
I was forced aware of graven faces.

Two chairs away his stark eyes
Unhidden by glasses
    since his are blind,
Now dependent on memoried places.

Near me sits a widow, yes, three times by death
Her coiffure and stylish attire
    accented by gifts
A clear alto voice—"I'll cling to that Old Cross."

Up front a young mother releases her restless
    child
to find another lap
    and yet another.
The honoree was her Nanna.

Late in entering a couple
whose togetherness of 60 years
    seems entwined in walkers
They push in slow rhythm.

The music,
technic-boxed
    lends background to a teen soloist,
"Our Father Who Art."

A tall, handsome minister, 20ish, rises reverently,
opening a flexible black leather Bible,
    an honorarium for recent graduation,
He slowly reads to us "I go to prepare a place."

Our nearness to that place,
either grave or urn marked,
    may be stayed or turned
at God's will.

A Cowboy Country Church
For James and Daisy

Hay, horses, hope, homemade
helped hitch their love.
"Together with their parents"
the invitation read.
"At seven on February 2, 2010"
Surrounded by friends
and varied families
One's brother read the vows;
Other's brother sang "Our Father . . ."
Together now
and forever.

"Love is friendship set to music"
Crossword clue

Eddie Anthony

Flying a plane before he drove a car
was portent for wide flight and service.
Just mark Venezuela, Columbia,
Brazil, Ecuador, Ghana, Peru,
Chile, Argentina, Africa,
Iceland, China and Japan.
Of these governments he reports Iceland
the most advanced in school
and Africa the most primitive.
Eddie's conversation remembers
campaign strategies and maneuvers
of the times he served in World War Two.
His skills seem foreign to our age.
Who among us has had
such wide exposure to war?
War memories do not fade.
Rather vividly they invade all else.

"But when the blast of war
Blows in our ears—
A terrible aspect."
William Shakespeare
1564-1616

Nuestro Princesa

She moves among us with a quietness that speaks.
Her attire, feminine dresses of azul, amarillo,
   rosado, or verde.
Her hair, au natural, tinged with gris wound round
   like a crown.
Her jewels, sterling or oro, maybe pearl or coral or
   aquamarine
Her voice, just above a whisper, is gestured by
   graceful hands.
Si. Si. To describe her you need a word more
   diminutive than petite.

Twas on Cinco de Mayo, a martes, at White Rock
   Courts festival
She with hair in queue tied with tortoise arrived at
   gaily adorned table.
He, her escort, White Rock's most gallant walker
   shares the gaiety.
We are glad they are among us—
Our ears respond as a Mariachi band of three bring
   music from strings
She strokes the braid across her throat in a Rapunzel
   moment.

A romantic knot—
Not forgotten—
In Mexico City—
We love her love stories.
Three?

Nancy and Bub Thompson

Nancy and Bub met on his 23[rd.]
'Twas 1937 at a
"Roll up the Rugs and Dance" party
"Let's dance."
"Oh my gosh—He's 6'3"
I'm 5'1"."

The moment's poignance
preceded 68 years
of love and fun.
They saw heights
in family of four,
photography career,
national and international travel.

Memories—
you should see her face
singing '40s songs—
"Ain't she sweet,"
"Ain't we got fun"

A low-key start
hit a high note.

Bertha Della Wimberly

The wee wisp of a woman weighing
  less than 100 lbs
  has lived 100 years.
Her memories, penned while prime
  are America's mirror.
She begins overseas with
  a blighted love-story flight,
  ancestor Theresa who'd not marry
  for less than love.
She threads her life through sentiment,
  stirring, "mind-boggling times."
The reward, "Through My Century"
  completed, edited, and published 2009.
She challenges us and her caring heirs to journal.
Through journaling love and happiness.

Mildred and J.Y. III
Love's Theme

Prologue: In her words the romance began simply, grew gradually, and became a validation of my poem, "Love's Theme."

"Love is a chance
Waiting to be
Connected
To the right voltage
Regardless of age."

We met at the mailbox in November 2001. I had moved here in March, one year after my husband died. He moved in October about five years after his wife died. So began five years of a wonderful relationship, partly because it was so unexpected, coming late in life. I was 79, he was 82. We enjoyed each other's company and were together constantly. To quote him, "We could tell each other anything", and we did. I never tired of his tales.

It's hard not to stare
When you see them.
"Ah—young love."
She with porcelain skin
He with nonchalant air
Sharing art, music, books, nature, their fare.
This gem, late-life love is rare.
Is it fate's facet?

Obituary

They are no more.
Obituaries declare so.
Carlyle says
"Biography is the only true history."
All biography is fruitful
Scriptural biography
Singularly so.
Biblical obituaries
Occur throughout Old and New Testament.
Perhaps the shortest but
Most beautiful obit
"He is risen"
Jerusalem A.D. 33
Matthew 28:7

Doc

Wry.
Funny.
Challenging.
Teasing.
Curious.
Intelligent
Offbeat.
Caring.
Compassionate.

A son's eulogy for a dad.
It's very common now—
To hear the child's take in
Eulogy or Obituary.
Did he know?
Was it evident always?

"No disguise can conceal love
Where it exists or feign it
Where it is lacking."
La Rochesacauld

My Terse Verse on 21st Vice

Sew, yes, sew again
So . . .
Sew with needle and thread.
Sew seams.
Shape garments.
Shame, first felt in Eden's garden unclothed,
Should be felt in today's bareness.
Shan't blame in such dareness of bareness
Show concern?
Surely, even a cape
Secures coverage of cleavage.
So, sew some seams.
Stress cover-up and restore modesty.
Save us from disaster.

Soak

Soak

Memory, you dry up
elusively
without saying
"see ya, aloha, or adieu."

Memory, please anchor a way
safely.
Stay without drift
names, places, actions.

Memory, find a trick
to selectively
protect, project, select.

Memory, soak up
carefully
where, when, who.

Memory, please retain
lively
talk, challenge, laughter.

So we olds won't "oblivionate",
saturate.

The Brain and the Heart

Our mental vein
isn't a topic in God's Word.
Brain isn't there as a word.
Our sustaining part
crops up often.
Both brain and heart
seem vital
for sustaining old age.
A pumping heart
without brain's thumping
dissolves humanity's usefulness.
It defines our loss of youthfulness.

A.M. or P.M.

The peel and sectioning of an orange
Early A.M. waiting for coffee to brew
has become sort of a symbol
in my old age—to just marvel at how it grew.

One morning, after a non-family Thanksgiving
my orange had pith and thick skin
as if it had had a hard time living—
uneven sections and sweetness very thin.

Knock. Knock. An unplanned visit that day
from family members not seen in years—
a teen fem and twenty, him who'd been away
came to say, "Gma, you're very dear."

He, with steady girl friend, absorbed in his work
she, just over a steady, ready for studies new
surprised their lonely oldie with a perk.
Rough times had polished how they grew.

The peel and sectioning of life
late P.M. battling for sleep
has become time to marvel,
as a nonagenarian, at life's sweep.

So, A.M. and P.M. peel and pith go
into shaping and making
oranges and youths to knock
on doors of wandering for them, wondering for
me.

Christmas Carding

That beautiful time of year
When we hear
From family, friends, new and far away
Nothing can compare with the magic
So special to our family
We do our own thing.

Christmas 2004

My Mississippi pine
     has brown and green needles
     at the same time.
Does it mean "Not all is fine
But growth refines us?" Transplanted from
Daddy's farm
Fourteen years ago. No cones
     until this year.
Seems to say, "The best is yet to come"—
Hope 'tis true for you and yours
     this New Year.

'Tis Christmas

His
birthday.
'Twas
a
Promise,
This
Child.
Read
Matthew,
Luke,
Isaiah.

The Computer's Fragility

Computer-savvy population.
Especially the young.
They begin even before Kg
To learn to point the mouse.
But you can louse it up.
   Delete
You'll lose it all.
   Virus
Infection feared. Insure against.
   Private
No secrets guarded by password.
   Fragile
Touch a button, gone; unretrievable.
Need sturdy protection from invaders.

Come-up-ance

It was Sister's 98th birthday.
We were celebrating very simply
Yet, with generous love to her.
Regretably I spoke an opinion
then tried to justify it.
Please, include my suggestion
as you consider finances.
"We know best.
This is our expertise."
Yet, I persisted.
So, a few harsh words.
"Off-the-bark conference."
Why, oh why, did I forget
the diminish age has?
Youthful skilled minds don't quiver.
My age has its shivers.
Deserved putdown
for a come-up-ance.

Genealogy

Chart of Recorded Descendants
ge
ne
al
o
gy
generation
next
allocate
ova
gynecological

Many study it, trace it, lace it
to notoriety or ruin
So what does it say?
Hmm,
The study stops with bloodline.
I'm the stop.
No next generation for us.
That's why daughters of adoptees
don't pursue.
So, do adoptee granddaughters
begin a new line?
It generates thought.

Hear, Here Is a Dear Bit o' Wit

Work for life on this earth
as if
You'll live forever in heaven
And work for life after
as if
You are to die tomorrow.

—*Queen Noor*
(She has both an East
and West attitude.)

Game Way

Acing it
keeps you young.
Stays aging
Delays dementia.
Connects friends,
Reflects ability.
Bridge bridges—
the river of doubt
About your presence.
Shuffle, deal, bid
Trumps or no trump
it'll keep you
out of the dumps.
Spades, hearts, diamonds, clubs.
How significantly named are the suits
for life's fruits:
The spade cultivates
The heart throbs
The diamond endures
The club wars.
Playing may then extend memory.

Old as a Verb

Old is a word that does
    oversize work as an adjective
    minimal work as a noun.
Yet, I want to make it a verb.

Kay, my most efficient and helpful
editor, nixed the idea.
She's not there yet.

For example, I'd say
"One olds the years by
Holding your own or
Else you'll be obsolete."

Old,
adj. 1. Far advanced in years or time
2. Of age
3. Also, olden former
4. Wise

n. 5. Former time

v. 6. Passes time

Good News for Modern Man

Hebrews, the New Testament book
whose authorship is disputed
speaks of God's
        prophets,
        angels,
        Father and Son.

"He also said, 'You, Lord in the beginning
        created the earth and with your own
        hands made the heavens. They will all
        disappear, but you will remain;

They will all grow old like clothes you will
        fold them up like a coat, and they will
        be changed like clothes.

You will fold them up like a coat and they will
        be changed like clothes.

But you are always the same, and you will
        never grow old.'"

Restaurant Ordering

"May I have half?"
"And I'll have the other half."

Just words of a couple,
old in years,
Alone now—after marriages to others.
So sharing again.
The taste of togetherness.

So, Go My Way

In my day
I heard
Billy Sunday
say, "Pay day
Someday".

In your day
you may hear
your mother say
"You obey today
or else."

Heed is the key.
Generation gap.

Purpose

We assume–

Seeds in overturned earth
makes us useful in God's plan
to use dirt.

Sowing, growing, weeding, tending
in acreage, lots, or pots
consumes us.

Seeds' births after rain
and relentless sun
gives us our crop (or flop).

Planting, your job or just joy,
yields sustenance–
body and spirit.

Lessons come from it
stems, stalks, vines, and trees,
as work in dirt.

Mine, this year, morning glories
Profuse vines growing heavenward
without a "glory."

No bloom.

"But what if I fail on my purpose here?
It is but to keep the nerves at strain.
To dry one's eyes and laugh at a fall,
And, baffled, get up and begin again."
–Robert Browning, 1812-1889

Life's Slice

Time is as adhesive as love,
Sticky, that is.
     Tick—Tick—
The clock moves
Sick, heartsick, lovesick,
     I've been.
Time and time again.
But it was only a crush
In the rush of time.
Spice in life's slice.

Old Yet Bold

Years have said it's time for you to fold.
My possessions are distributed or sold
My goodbye to duties has been told
My omissions and sins have had their scold.
And, here I am on life's new threshold.

These circumstances seem so cold
I'll have to search for friendship's gold
'Cause my lifestyle wasn't made in this mold.
I'm praying that my anchor will hold
When my name's the one for whom the bell has
    tolled.

Photos

James, me, Jon
My sons
It may be that we were apart for a time
so that we could be back together for all time
(Philemon 1:15), God's Word.

My beloved parents' 50th
BIBLE, Wash—1872-1964
BIBLE, Alice—1884-1968
"The woman's cause is man's: they rise or sink together."
—Alfred Lord Tennyson, 1809-1892

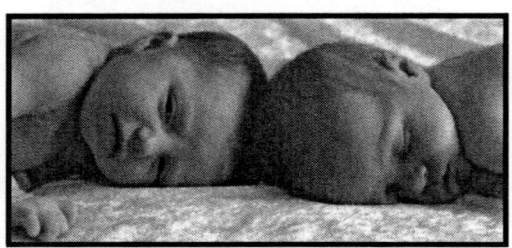

The W.N. Bible family bloodline continues.
Above, twins Clare Catherine and Connor Patrick Colburn
Both came together as gifts of God,
so "Light tomorrow with today."
—Elizabeth Barrett Browning, 1806-1861

Me and great-grand, Taylor Smith, Bryant and Jennifer's child
93 years, 6 years
"I got a shock hearing the grown-ups talk to find that
my Grandmother's name wasn't her name at all,
only her married name."
—Carol Ann Duffy, Poet Laureate 2009-our first family poet

Our happy togetherness on the coldest of nights.
Cathy, J.D., Kristina, Daisy, James, Jon, me
2/2/2010
"All love at first–proves the pleasanter the colder."
—Samuel Butler, 1612-1680

The Hill family fems
Catherine, 99; Lu, aunt;
Andrea, mom; Belinda,
grandmother; and Claire
Catherine, 6 months.
Not pictured: Kate and
Stephanie, aunts.
"Queen rose of the rosebud
garden of girls."
—Alfred Lord Tennyson,
1809-1892

Landen and Alys Jewels
Great-grandson,
Granddaughter
"O aching time.
O moments big as years."
—John Keats, 1795-1821

Hailey, 8; Jayce, 9; Alys and
Jay Dill; Bryce, 5.
Pronounced a family
3/20/2010
Grains of sand blended in crystal
"To see a world in a grain of
sand, And a Heaven in a wild
flower, Hold Infinity in the
palm of your hand, And
Eternity in an hour."
—William Blake, 1757-1827

Christmas 2005
My first away from neighbors
Betty and John Crain in 35 years
"*Love thy neighbor as
thyself*"
(Mt. 19:19).

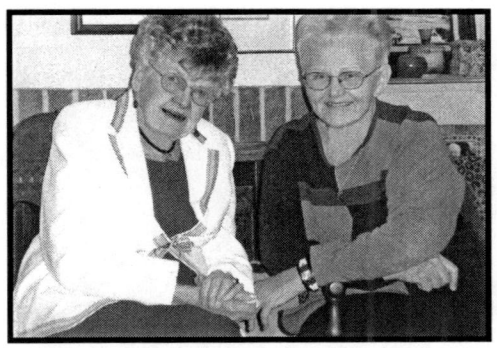

God did not give me a birth daughter—he gave Lana
Me with her on 3/3/07
From my high-school favorite
"For the dear God who loveth us
He made and loveth all."
—Rime of the Ancient Mariner, Samuel Taylor Coleridge, 1772-1834

Carol Hittson Kent and Elizabeth Hittson
Carol, my former student, a Texas legislator
Her mother, book club for 40 years—still reading.
"A friend may well be reckoned the masterpiece of Nature."
—Ralph Waldo Emerson, 1803-1882

Elizabeth May, me, and Bertha's book, *Through My Century*
Together we worked on the manuscript.
"When a new book is published, read an old one."
—Theodore Roethbe, 1908-1963

Me in Washington, D.C. after 57 years; Our retired teachers organization won
national honors; Teaching has many rewards—here a red wagon
from Colin Powell, retired Secretary of State
"Why me, Lord, still living?"
—MBS

Mac and Lolita Green at citizenship party
He, a local
She, from the Philippines
I'm her third Mom (She has hers, his, and me.)
Email love across the Pacific
"O Love, the ocean cross
just see us together
now and forever."
—MBS

Karen and Jon Smith 7/31/2009
On Florida waters
"I must down to the seas again, for the call of the running tide
is a wild call and a clear call that may not be denied."
—John Masefield, 1878-1967

Marie Davis, my sidekick, travel companion,
reading buddy, and soulmate, reads DMN's O's.
"—rest of thy bones' and soul's delivery."
—John Donne 1571-1631

The living tree planted June 20, 1987 in Jerusalem by the Fleischer family
in memory of my husband.
"And when ye shall come into the land and ye shall plant . . . "
(Lev. 19:23).

My son, James, 4, climbing on a replica of Rodin's statue,
The Thinker. This statue has been a significant part of my life. On
my retirement I gave the statue to Garland Independent School
District, for which I worked for 31 years.
It now sits in the courtyard of Garland High School.
"Cheerfully, then, my little man, live and laugh as boyhood can."
—John Whittier (1807-1892)

LaVergne, TN USA
31 August 2010
195304LV00001B/1/P